MW00917850

Ray Bradbury's

Fahrenheit 451

BookCaps Study Guide

www.bookcaps.com

Table of Contents

Historical Context

Ray Bradbury (1920-) is a distinguished and prolific science fiction writer, probably best known for his futuristic novel *Fahrenheit 451*. The title refers to the temperature at which paper burns. Bradbury first wrote the short story *The Fireman* in 1951 for the magazine *Galaxy Science Fiction*. Bradbury expanded the story and published *Fahrenheit 451* in 1953.

Scholars often link the novel to the historic backdrop of 1950s America. Some see the book, written soon after World War II, as a response to censorship practiced by the Nazi regime. Others cite Senator Joseph McCarthy's investigations into evidence of Communism among the creative elite. According to Bradbury, one must not look further than the rise of television for the true inspiration.

Bradbury has been vocal about the often-misinterpreted novel. He insists the novel is not about government censorship. Rather, the book's moral warns of the dumbing down of people through television. Television and radio, according to Bradbury, informs its viewers of "factoids" rather than ideas.

Unlike other novels of the dystopian genre, the people willingly agree to live under such conditions. Bradbury envisions a society of minorities, so easily offended, that gradually all literary material is labeled as distasteful. The populace opts instead for inoffensive, vanilla television for entertainment. The people stop reading and only then does the government employ censorship. In addition, Bradbury added a coda to the 1979 paperback edition. The coda rants against editors and readers suggesting censorship of his novels in the name of political correctness.

Plot Overview

Guy Montag is a fireman. In the future, firemen do not put out fires. They start them.

Books are illegal, and libraries are burned, along with the homes where they are found. Most people do not miss literature and instead spend their days listening to the radio or watching unintelligent television programming.

Montag begins to question his life after a series of events. First, he meets a peculiar young girl, full of questions and unusual behavior. She would rather spend the day with nature than in front of the television. The whimsical curiosity of the young girl greatly affects Montag. Then, one day she disappears.

Saddened by the loss of a new friend, Montag answers a call to burn an illegal library. The owner refuses to leave her books and burns to death with them. Montag is appalled by the episode, wondering what could be inside the some 20 books he has stolen from sites over the years.

After showing his wife the hidden library, she reports him. Demoralized, Montag is forced to extinguish his own home. Afterward, the fire captain threatens to visit Montag's ally. Montag murders him and fleas with the remaining books, his dramatic pursuit televised. He finds a group of roaming intellectuals who memorize books in the hope the words can be revived one day. Shortly after his escape, the city is demolished by war. The group hopes the destruction will provide the opening to rebuild civilization based on deeper ideals.

Themes

Censorship

In Bradbury's world, books are outlawed. As a fireman, Montag burns illegal books and the houses in which they are found. A variety of factors led up to this government control. As population explodes, more groups of minorities develop, taking issue with literature that offends them. In addition, television and radio provide entertainment requiring less concentration and intellectual work. Information overload also played a role in people retreating to their parlor rooms. Ultimately, Bradbury says, the people invited censorship by deciding to not read books. Books became briefer until they disappeared altogether. Only when the people stopped reading did the government forbid them.

Suicide

After her overdose, technicians arrive to pump Mildred's stomach. It is a common occurrence, they say dispassionately, smoking cigarettes. The firemen mention that one poor soul programmed the mechanical hound to hunt his own chemical balance, resulting in a gruesome suicide. Later, Captain Beatty does not fight Montag's threats of murder, leading Montag to presume Beatty wanted to die. And in a key moment of the novel, a woman uses her own match to burn herself with her books rather than give up her illegal library. In a society that caters to universal happiness, for many in the novel, the happiness proves to be empty.

Technology

At the Montag home, Mildred watches television that spans three walls. She bugs Montag to spring for a fourth. The walls even allow her to interact with characters. If she is not watching television, she has "Seashell Radios" stuffed in her ears. Faber gives Montag a similar invention that allows two-way communication. Cars drive at extraordinary speed. The mechanical hound hunts and demolishes its prey programmed to target a specific scent. Bradbury's world, created in the 1950s, includes many examples of advanced technology. He highlights the negative consequences of technology, culminating in the destruction of the city by bombardment.

Television

In Bradbury's world, television has replaced intellectual thought and meaningful, personal relationships. Mildred watches television constantly and refers to the characters as "family". She cares more about these relatives than Montag, whom she shows little love. Montag tells Faber that television "is real" for Mildred. "It tells you what to think and blasts it in," he says. The rise of television led to the censorship of books because the people chose television over books. In that decision, the people chose a more superficial world as television provides only "factoids", leaving more complex concepts unearthed.

Anti-Intellectualism

Faber is an out-of-work professor due to lack of interest in the liberal arts. He is an outcast, as is Granger and Clarisse. Beatty recalls the high school days of hating on the smart kid. The sediment becomes policy, as intellectual "snobs" are closely watched by the government. According to Beatty, "the word intellectual became the swear word it deserved to be." No one wants to be made to feel less intelligent, and, therefore, firemen serve as "custodians of our peace of mind, the focus of our understandable and rightful dread of being inferior," says Beatty.

Happiness

At the end of their first meeting, Clarisse asks Montag if he is happy. Puzzled by the question, he returns home to find his wife has overdosed. What at first seems like a ridiculous question takes on new meaning for Montag. Society's main motive for state-sponsored censorship is to keep everyone happy and unoffended. However, with suicide so common, it is evident that the happiness is not genuine. In a world where the people have institutionalized the idea of "ignorance is bliss", anyone who would challenge this is seen as impending on happiness and is disposed.

Political Correctness

Beatty explains the origin of censorship to Montag. As population explodes, so do the minority groups, who take offense to anything that fails to put them in a less than positive light. "Don't step on the toes of the dog lovers, the cat lovers, doctors, lawyers, merchants....," Beatty says. In his coda added to the 1979 paperback edition, Bradbury retaliates against those recommending he change his books to fit a more politically correct vision. "There is more than one way to burn a book," he writes. "And the world is full of people running about with lit matches."

Death

Most of the characters in the book die. Clarisse falls victim to a speeding car. Montag murders Beatty. The old woman burns herself rather than give up her books. Most of the other characters are presumed dead when the city is leveled. Beyond the physical deaths lies the paradox of living. At one point, Montag reflects on the irony of referring to the room with the television as the "living room". Montag gradually comes to believe the emptiness of life has led to a society of the walking dead, lacking the deep relationships and meaning required to feel alive.

Programming

The mechanical hound is programmed to hunt its prey based on chemical disposition. Montag speculates as to whether the robot likes him. "It doesn't like or dislike. It just functions," says Beatty. "It doesn't think anything we don't want it to think." The government exercises similar control over the people. For example, no one talks about the war. Mrs. Phelps does not worry about her solider husband because the President insists the coming battle will be a quick victory. Such programming is made easier when everyone is distracted with entertainment, mainly television programming.

Distraction

When Montag speaks to Mildred, she never gives him her full attention. Her mind is always at least partially devoted to the television or radio. The people of this society are constantly being distracted from reality and are tricked into thinking that the entertainment is "real". When Montag tries to read a book on the subway, he struggles to block out the commercial jingle playing over the speaker system. In this world, constant, loud stimulation makes it nearly impossible to concentrate. This way, the people are not thinking about more important things, such as the impending war or the infringements on freedom.

Characters

Guy Montag

The protagonist is a fireman charged with enforcing government oppression by burning illegal books. Throughout the novel, he grows increasingly disgruntled with the superficial society and his role in state sponsored censorship. Doubts are intensified after meeting a young, inquisitive girl and witnessing a woman chose to burn to death with her books. After revealing his own hidden library to his wife, Montag is ordered to burn his own home. He murders the fire captain and runs, prompting a dramatic televised police chase. He escapes and finds a group of wandering intellectuals who memorize books.

Mildred Montag

Montag's wife Mildred is not unlike many. Her life revolves around mindless entertainment. She often has radio speakers stuffed in her ears or watches her "family" on three walls of television. Mildred's true happiness comes in to question when she overdoses on sleeping pills. She does not remember the episode the next day, nor is she concerned. Montag and Mildred show little affection or empathy toward each other. Neither can remember when or where they met, and Mildred does not seem to care. When Montag shows her the books he has stolen, she betrays him by reporting the library.

Clarisse McClellan

Montag meets his new neighbor Clarisse on his way to work one night. While at first uneasy around the strange girl, the two develop a fast friendship. The carefree 17-year-old is more interested in nature and talking to people than watching television. She describes herself as "crazy", and is forced to see a psychiatrist for her "anti-social" behavior. At their first meeting, she asks Montag if he is happy. The question has a profound effect on Montag. Clarisse along with her questions serve as a catalyst for Montag's voyage of self-discovery. Later, Clarisse dies when he is hit by a car.

Technicians

Montag comes home one night to find his wife, Mildred, has overdosed on sleeping pills. Montag calls the paramedics and two cigarette-smoking technicians arrive. They haul in a machine that pumps her stomach and provides a complete blood transfusion. They explain that such calls are a regular occurrence. Montag is struck by the fact that the two are not doctors, and secondly by how nonchalant they both are. The impersonal technicians appear to have little sympathy or decorum, a common attribute in the novel. The incident haunts Montag throughout the novel.

Captain Beatty

Montag's boss at the firehouse suspects Montag of wrongdoing. The proud fire captain lectures Montag on the rationale for firemen and the pitfalls of giving into curiosity and stealing books. Using literary references in his arguments, he insists there is no value in books. The fireman's role is to ensure that everyone remains happy and comfortable, he says. Later, the men arrive at Montag's house to burn his illegal library. After Beatty forces him to burn his own house, Montag murders him with a flamethrower. Montag later concludes that Beatty wanted to die.

Faber

Montag meets Faber in the park about a year before the story takes place. Montag knows Faber has a book under his coat as the two converses, but Montag does nothing about it. Faber becomes comfortable enough to quote poetry and give Montag his contact information. Montag remembers the unemployed professor when he feels he has no one else to turn to. Faber gives him a two-way radio he invented so the two can communicate. While on the lam, Montag apologizes for involving him. Faber is delighted to help, however, and tells him he feels alive again working for the cause he was always to frighten to support.

Granger

Granger is the apparent leader of the wandering group of intellectuals that Montag meets after fleeing the city. The scholar encourages Montag to recall the words of his chosen book, as the members all memorize a piece of literature. He puts confidence in the idea that everyone who has made a difference in the world can be deemed important. Montag listens to this and wonders what Mildred has done that could ever be considered important. As the novel closes, Granger leads the group to rebuild civilization after witnessing the city be destroyed.

Mrs. Phelps and Mrs. Bowles

Mildred's friends arrive one evening to watch television. Montag angrily shuts the parlor walls off and asks Mrs. Phelps about the impending war. Mrs. Phelps says she is not worried about her solider husband and shows little affection for him. Mrs. Bowles displays a similar affinity for her children, allowing the parlor walls to do the babysitting. The two voted for the current president because he was the more handsome of the two candidates. Montag reads a poem to the two ladies, after which Mrs. Phelps cries. Mrs. Bowles scolds Montag for upsetting her and the two report the books.

Black and Stoneman

Montag's two fellow firemen willfully perform their duties in burning illegal books. When Montag questions whether firemen ever put out fires rather than start them, Black and Stoneman pull out their rule books and show him the blurb about the Firemen of America's founding by Ben Franklin to burn English-influenced books. When the firemen show up at Montag's house to burn his illegal library, Montag threatens the two with a flamethrower and knocks them out. On his way to Faber's house, he plants books in Black's house and phones in an alarm.

Woman with library

The firemen rush to what should be a routine call to burn an illegal library. As the firemen crash the place, Montag steals a book. He begs the woman with the library to leave the house before it is set ablaze. She refuses to leave, lighting her own kitchen match, burning herself with her books. Montag is left physically ill by the situation. The episode leaves Montag wondering what could possibly be inside those pages that could spark so much defiance. It is a defining moment that pushes Montag over the edge.

Mechanical Hound

With eight insect-like legs, the mechanical hound is set to track a person's specific chemical balance and inject its prey with a numbing needle. The hound thinks only what it is programmed to think, according to Beatty. Montag suspects the hound is programmed to growl at him, but Beatty discounts his suspicions. Beatty, however, sends the hound sniffing around the house to warn Montag. Later, Montag destroys the hound with a flamethrower, but not before the hound injects him with its needle. Later, the authorities release another hound, but Montag throws off his scent and escapes.

Part 1: The Hearth and the Salamander

At first glance, Guy Montag appears to enjoy his job. With the number 451 emblazoned on his helmet, he finds pleasure in his destructive vocation. Modern buildings may be fireproof, but the role of the fireman has evolved rather than become obsolete. Firemen start fires. Firemen, like Montag, are charged with the task of burning books.

It takes a conversation with an unusual 17-year-old to introduce a sense of unease into Montag's complacency. At their first meeting, Clarisse McClellan describes herself as "crazy", because she does "crazy" things like sit around and talks with her family members. Even though many fear fireman, Clarisse does not fear Montag. She asks Montag if firemen used to extinguish fires rather than start them. He laughs at the thought.

Clarisse is odd. She would rather walk in the night air and smell things than watch television. Most people enjoy television and driving so fast, they miss the beauty around them, she says. According to her uncle, billboards used to be 20-feet wide, as opposed to 200-feet wide, because people did not use to drive so fast. At first uneasy, Montag becomes charmed by his inquisitive new neighbor. Before parting, Clarisse asks Montag if he is happy. This question haunts him as he returns home.

Montag arrives home to find his wife, Mildred, overdosed on sleeping pills. Technicians arrive with a machine that pumps her stomach and gives her a blood transfusion. The disinterested technicians indicate that such calls are common and the procedure routine. In the morning, Mildred does not remember the night before and appears unconcerned.

Mildred represents the typical citizen of Bradbury's grim vision of the future America. She spends her days listening to the "Seashell Radios" stuffed in her ears and watching three walls of television in the parlor room. Technology allows her to interact with televised people, whom she refers to as her relatives.

On his way to work, Montag encounters Clarisse again. This time, she introduces doubts regarding his love for his wife. In addition, Clarisse tells Montag that she sees a psychiatrist because she displays "anti-social" behavior, such as hiking, bird watching, collecting butterflies, and simply sitting and thinking. Clarisse then questions him about why he became a fireman and receives no answer.

At the firehouse, Montag studies the mechanical hound with its eight legs. The firemen can program the robotic hound to target a particular chemical balance and inject numbing chemicals with a large needle. The hound growls menacingly at Montag, prompting him to speculate as to whether the hound was programmed to do so. Captain Beatty discounts his concerns, sensing a bit of guilt from Montag.

Meetings with Clarisse become routine over the next week. Montag finds their conversations relaxing. Then one day, she is gone, leaving Montag to worry.

At the firehouse, Montag asks what happened to the man whose books they burned the week before. Beatty answers that the man was sent to an insane asylum. He then asks if firemen were ever charged with putting out fires rather than starting them. The other men take out their rulebooks and remind him of an excerpt that says the Firemen of America was established in 1790 by Benjamin Franklin to burn English-influenced books.

The bell rings and the firemen race to a new location. They ransack the place, gathering books and magazines for the blaze. In the confusion, Montag finds himself stealing a book. Returning to his duty, Montag begs the owner to leave the home. The woman refuses to leave, opting instead to burn with her books. She pulls out her own match and lights the kerosene-soaked books.

Rattled by the experience, Montag wonders what could possibly be in those books that would be worth dying. He returns home obviously shaken, hiding the stolen book under his pillow. In bed, Montag asks Mildred when and where they met. Neither could remember. Montag finds this troubling. Mildred deems it unimportant as she swallows more sleeping pills. He remembers the night she overdosed and questions if he would have cried had she died.

Later, Montag asks Mildred about the neighbor girl Clarisse. Mildred says she forgot to tell him that the girl was hit by a car and killed. The family moved away. Montag cannot believe she forgot to tell him this. Later that night, Montag senses the hound preying outside the house.

The next day, Montag feels sick and does not go to work. The smell of kerosene makes him vomit. Mildred shows little compassion for the sickly Montag, even after he tells her about the burning woman. He asks her how she would feel if he quit his job for a while. Mildred is furious at the suggestion that one woman's death is worth giving up a job.

Surprisingly, Captain Beatty arrives, seemingly aware of Montag's increasing misgivings toward his job. He comes prepared to lecture on the history of his profession. Beatty explains that as population explodes, minority groups form that may take issue with literature. Montag listens, the stolen book still hidden under his pillow. Mildred attempts to adjust his pillow and Montag struggles to keep her away from the hidden plunder. Beatty continues: Books do not agree with each other and thus fail to tell a coherent narrative of inarguable facts. "Slippery" subjects such as philosophy fall out of favor, along with liberal arts college enrollment. Anti-intellectualism reigns, with inoffensive television taking the place of books. The goal of the firemen is to keep people happy and comfortable, safe from "conflicting theory."

Mildred finally finds the hidden book and reacts, but leaves the room as the two firemen continue the conversation. Beatty says every fireman is tempted to steal a book, but there is nothing of value inside.

When firemen are caught stealing a book, they are given 24 hours to burn it.

After Beatty leaves, Montag feels compelled to show his wife some 20 books he has stolen over the years. Mildred panics. Montag insists on looking at them. If Beatty is correct and they provide no value, they will burn them together. Someone comes to the door again, but the two do not answer.

Part 2: The Sieve and the Sand

Montag skims through the books frantically trying to find meaning. He often connects passages to his dead neighbor. Mildred acts uninterested and resists helping her husband, calling books unreal. Meanwhile, Montag see signs of the hound prowling outside the house, which Mildred identifies as a dog. Mildred worries about the consequences of reading the books and insists she receives more meaning from her "family" on the parlor walls.

Bombers cross the skies above the house as they do every hour, prompting Montag to wonder aloud why no one talks about America's wars. Rumors say that while American society has its fun and riches, parts of the world starve and garner hatred for America. Montag's speech is interrupted by the phone and Mildred dives into a mindless conversation about a television show. At this moment, Montag appears to give up on Mildred. His mind races for someone else to turn to.

Suddenly, he remembers a chance encounter in the park about a year ago. There, he saw an old man quickly hide something in his coat. The man attempted to flee, and Montag stopped him. The old man defiantly declared his innocence, but Montag calmed him with some small talk. The man turned out to be a retired English professor who was out of work due to the lack of interest in the liberal arts. The professor, named Faber, eased gradually throughout the one-hour conversation, even quoting poetry. Montag suspected Faber of hiding a book under his coat, but was not interested in exposing the professor.

Before parting, Faber provided Montag with his contact information.

Based on the listing at the firehouse, Montag had come to suspect that he was in possession of the last copy of the Bible and other books. He calls Faber and zealously interrogates him. Faber anxiously confirms Montag's suspicions and hangs up on him. Montag decides he must leave to make a copy of the Bible before returning the original to Beatty. Before leaving, Montag asks Mildred if her parlor wall "family" loves her. She is confused by the question.

On the subway, Montag sits with the book in full view. He wonders if he could memorize from the book. The daunting task reminds him of a time as a child he tried to fill a sieve with sand, because a teasing cousin had promised him a dime to do it. He studies the book, only to have his concentration broken by a commercial jingle being played over the speaker system. His frustration turns to spectacle and his fellow passengers distance themselves from the crazed man.

Montag arrives at Faber's house. Faber is reluctant to allow him in until Montag swears he is alone. Inside, Montag tells Faber that he stole the book that Faber is eager to examine. Turning the pages, Faber reflects on the current portrayal of Christ on television as a sugarcoated product peddler. Faber also confesses inaction against the crackdown on books, calling himself a coward. In turn, Montag expresses his growing dissatisfaction with the emptiness of modern life, false happiness, and his desire to find answers in books. He begs Faber to teach him to understand the significance of what he reads. Faber explains societal woes go beyond the elimination of books, adding that television could present similar intellectual curiosity instead of the unintelligent programming. He continues, saying books "are full of pores", or tell deeper truths that may make people uncomfortable, which is what society needs: "quality, texture of information." Society also needs leisure, or time to reflect on information, according to Faber. Finally, individuals require the right to act on this new information.

The two hatch a plan to plant books in firemen's houses. The plan is soon rejected as lacking the interest to distract the public from the mindless parlor walls. Faber suggests Montag leave, to which he responds by ripping out pages of the Bible, much to the horror of Faber. Montag continues tearing, insisting Faber help him. Faber finally agrees to connect Montag with a printer. Before Montag leaves, Faber provides his invention that is similar to a "Seashell Radio" that allows the two to communicate.

War propaganda plays on the radio as Montag goes to the bank to retrieve money for the printer. Later that evening, Mrs. Phelps and Mrs. Bowles arrive to watch television with Mildred. Annoyed with the loud and ridiculous programming, Montag shuts off the walls, leaving the room silent. He asks about the impending war. Mrs. Phelps says she is not worried about her solider husband as the battle should be a quick victory. Mildred tries to redirect the conversation back to television, but Montag presses on, asking about the women's children. Mrs. Bowles allows the parlor walls to do most of the parenting. Regarding politics, the women voted for the current president because he was more handsome than the other candidate.

This infuriates Montag. He exits the room and returns with a book of poetry. From the earpiece, Faber's voice pleads him to stop. Shocked, Mildred attempts to defuse the situation by explaining that once a year firemen are allowed to bring a book home to see how silly they are. Faber urges Montag to go along with the lie, and Montag reluctantly agrees to do so. Mildred encourages Montag to read a poem to the ladies for a laugh. He proceeds to read a poem called *Dover Beach.* After finishing the poem, Mrs. Phelps was crying. Mrs. Bowles scolds Montag for upsetting her, confirming her belief that poetry leads to sadness. Montag then burns the book, but it is not enough for the women to stay. Montag lambastes the women as they leave with scathing personal attacks, ordering them to go home.

Montag finds that some of the books are missing and assumes Mildred has begun to dispose of them. He hides the rest in the backyard and heads to work. Montag turns in a book to Captain Beatty and joins his card game. Beatty quotes literature to try to arouse a response out of Montag, who remains quiet with the urging of Faber. The game is interrupted by the alarm, and Montag grudgingly prepares. When they arrive, Montag discovers they have come to his home.

Part 3: Burning Bright

Montag is in disbelief as he and Beatty stand outside Montag's home. Beatty asks why Montag continued to harbor books even after he sent the mechanical hound to sniff around the house. Muttering to herself, Mildred leaves carrying a suitcase and disappears into a taxi and out of his life. Seeing torn books on the ground, Montag assumes Mildred had seen him hide the books in the backyard and taken them inside.

Beatty pokes at Montag, calling him a fool for thinking he would not get caught. He orders Montag to burn his house with a flamethrower. He complies and enjoys the act, receiving pleasure in burning the parlor room and other remnants of his former life. As the fire blazed, Beatty tells Montag that he will be under arrest once he is done.

Still holding the flamethrower, Montag asks Beatty if Mildred was the one who called in the alarm. Beatty nods adding that he let previous calls from her friends slide. Resuming his speech, Beatty demands to know why he did it. Receiving no answer, Beatty strikes Montag, dislodging the radio. Beatty picks the small earpiece off the ground and says they will trace it and pay his friend a visit. In response, Montag switches the safety catch on the flamethrower. This catches Beatty by surprise, but he soon recovers with a smile, requesting a pretentious final speech and daring him to pull the trigger. "We never burned *right*...," Montag says before showering Beatty with flames. The other two firemen are silent as Beatty is reduced to ashes. Montag aims the flamethrower, orders them to turn around, and knocks them out. The mechanical hound leaps out of the night at Montag, and he catches the hound with a blast of fire, but not before the hound injects his massive needle, numbing his leg.

Montag struggles to his feet and limps forward in great pain, cursing his recent actions. He returns to the backyard and finds four books Mildred had not moved. He takes the books as sirens are heard. He hobbles for a while and collapses in an alley. Motionless, he sobs at the thought that Beatty wanted to die, and he was the one to kill him. He struggled up as he hears hurried footsteps. He heads toward Faber's house. Listening to his Seashell Radio, he hears reports of the pursuit with reports on the brewing war. Crossing a boulevard, a car races toward him. Thinking it may be a cop car, Montag breaks into a sprint, stumbles and drops a book. The car swerves and blazes down the street. He concludes that the car was driven by kids aiming to hit him for entertainment, only avoiding him once he fell fearing the impact would roll the car. Thinking the fall saved his life, he continues to the house of a fellow fireman where he plants books and calls in an alarm.

Montag reaches Faber's house and tells him what happened, not entirely believing it himself. He reflects on his life changing before his eyes. He is apologetic for involving Faber, but Faber says he feels alive again working for the cause. Montag gives Faber 100 dollars. Faber suggests Montag follow the river to railroad tracks where he heard camps of intellectuals roam. The two could reunite in St. Louis, where Faber is heading soon to meet a retired printer. Faber and Montag check a small television and see his name being plastered. They learn that a new mechanical hound has joined the chase. Montag instructs Faber to disinfect the house, burn the furniture, and turn on the air conditioner and sprinklers to kill the trail. He also takes a suitcase of Faber's dirtiest clothes.

Montag runs. He runs past windows, seeing people watch Faber's house on the parlor walls. He also sees the hound sniff and forge ahead on his trail. Over the Seashell Radio, he hears the announcer encouraging everyone to look outside on the count of ten to spot the fugitive. As the announcer reaches ten, he finds the river. He changes into Faber's clothes and swims. The hound and helicopters reach the river and lose his trail. He floats down the calming water, feeling free to think.

The water guides him to shore. Soon, he finds the railroad tracks. He believes Clarisse has walked here before. After walking some time, he sees a flickering fire in the distance. He approaches to find people. He stands in the trees until he is invited inside. Granger, the apparent leader of the group, refers to Montag by his name. He offers a drink that will change his chemical index. The camp has a portable TV and had been expecting Montag. Granger informs Montag that the chase continues on television. Police zero in on an innocent scapegoat on a walk. Granger says the authorities need to save face after losing Montag at the river. The televised chase needed a satisfying climax, as well. The evening stroller no doubt had been known by the authorities, as such behavior was odd. Montag screams as the hound tackles the innocent. Montag is dead, the announcer says.

Following the traumatic scene on television, Granger introduces him to the various intellectuals of the camp. He asks Montag what he has to offer. He answers the *Book of Ecclesiastes*, but only his fuzzy memory of it. Granger is delighted and explains that each person remembers literature, a living record of history being passed down through generations. Granger is Plato's *Republic*. The group waits for the war to start and quickly end, and maybe after they will be of some use to the rebuilding society.

Jets approach the city. Knowing destruction is imminent, Montag remembers Mildred. Granger says people leave a memorable fingerprint on the world that lives on. Montag cannot remember anything good Mildred would leave. Then in an instant, the city is flattened. Montag knows Faber would be en route to more destruction, and Mildred is dead. It is then he remembers where they met: Chicago. The power of the explosions knocks the group over.

The next morning, Montag and Granger watch bacon sizzle in the pan. Granger mentions the Phoenix, an ancient bird that burns and rises again from its ashes. The group head to the ashes of the city for resurrection, as Montag remembers pieces of the *Book of Ecclesiastes*.

About BookCaps

We all need refreshers every now and then. Whether you are a student trying to cram for that big final, or someone just trying to understand a book more, BookCaps can help. We are a small, but growing company, and are adding titles every month.

Visit www.bookcaps.com to see more of our books. Or contact us with any questions.

Cover Image by © Sergej Khackimullin - Fotolia

Made in the USA
Lexington, KY
17 July 2013